ladies
of Jazz

Alphabetical Contents List

Body And Soul - 4

Don't Explain - 47

Ev'ry Time We Say Goodbye - 34

The Lady Is A Tramp - 42

Little Girl Blue - 62

Love Me Or Leave Me - 50

Mad About The Boy - 18

The Man I Love - 14

Manhattan - 38

Misty - 66

My Baby Just Cares For Me - 53

Night And Day - 9

September In The Rain - 26

Smoke Gets In Your Eyes - 69

What A Diff'rence A Day Made - 30

Body And Soul

Words by Frank Eyton, Edward Heyman and Robert Sour
Music by Johnny Green

Contents

Billie Holiday

Body And Soul - 4
The Man I Love - 14
Night And Day - 9

Dinah Washington

Mad About The Boy - 18
September In The Rain - 26
What A Diff'rence A Day Made - 30

Ella Fitzgerald

Ev'ry Time We Say Goodbye - 34
The Lady Is A Tramp - 42
Manhattan - 38

Nina Simone

Don't Explain - 47
Love Me Or Leave Me - 50
My Baby Just Cares For Me - 53

Sarah Vaughan

Little Girl Blue - 62
Misty - 66
Smoke Gets In Your Eyes - 69

IMP

International
MUSIC
Publications

© International Music Publications Limited
Griffin House 161 Hammersmith Road London W6 8BS

Published 1999

Production: Sadie Cook
Cover design: The London Advertising Partnership
Cover photos used courtesy of Redferns Music
Picture Library

Reproducing this music in any form is illegal and forbidden by the
Copyright, Designs and Patents Act 1988

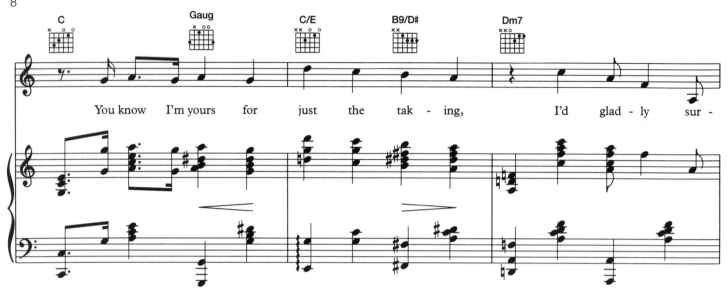

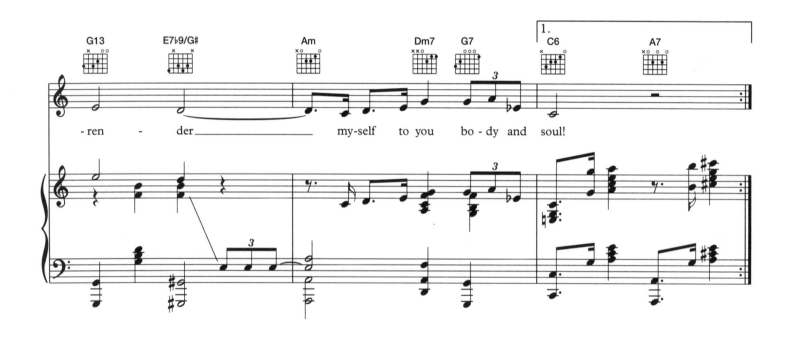

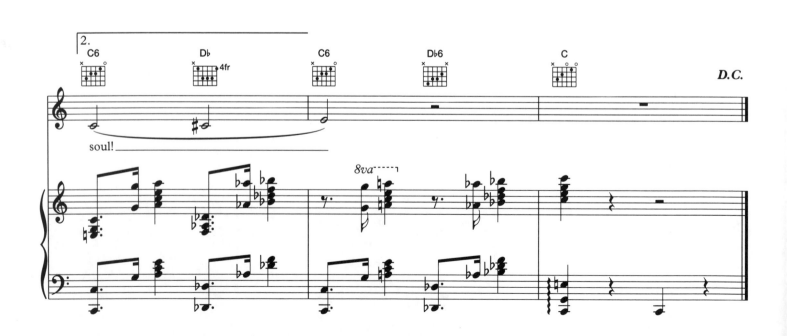

Night And Day

Words and Music by Cole Porter

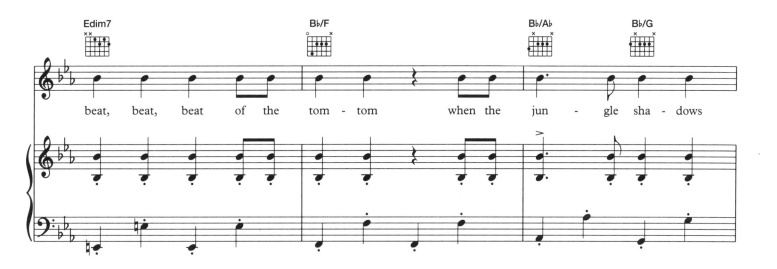

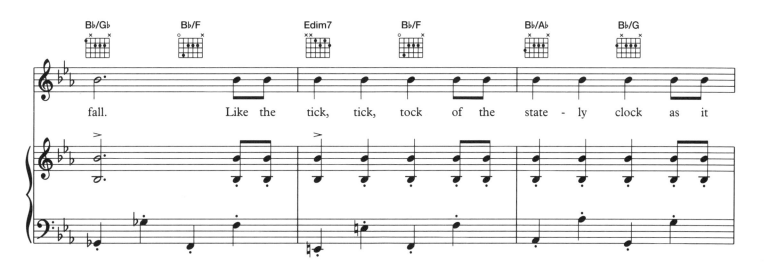

The Man I Love

Music and Lyrics by George Gershwin and Ira Gershwin

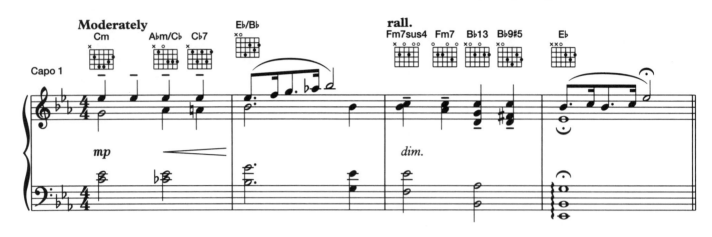

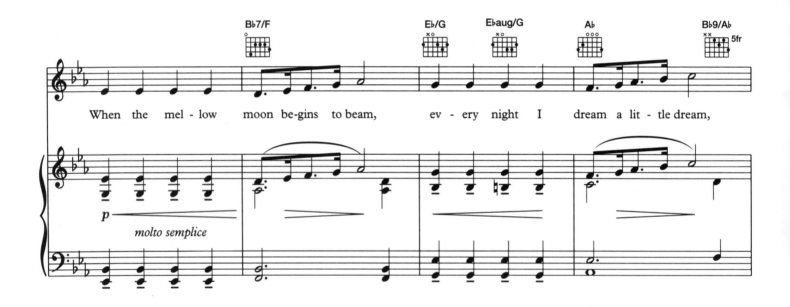

When the mel-low moon be-gins to beam, ev-ery night I dream a lit-tle dream,

and of course Prince Charm-ing is the theme, the he for me. Al -

Mad About The Boy

Words and Music by Noël Coward

22

23

September In The Rain

Words by Al Dubin
Music by Harry Warren

What A Difference A Day Made

Words and Music by Maria Grever
English Words by Stanley Adams

Ev'ry Time We Say Goodbye

Words and Music by Cole Porter

When you're near———— there's such an air of spring———— a-bout it

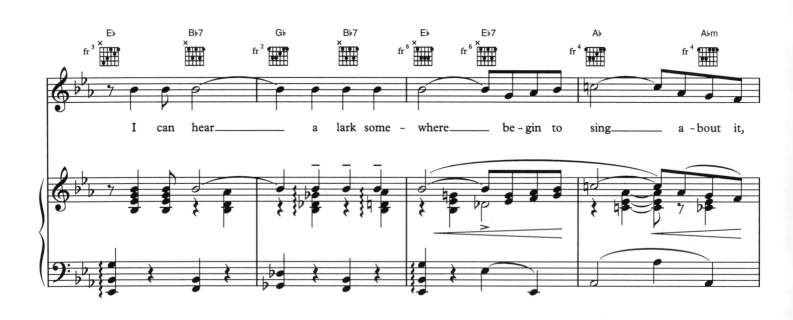

I can hear———— a lark some - where———— be-gin to sing———— a-bout it,

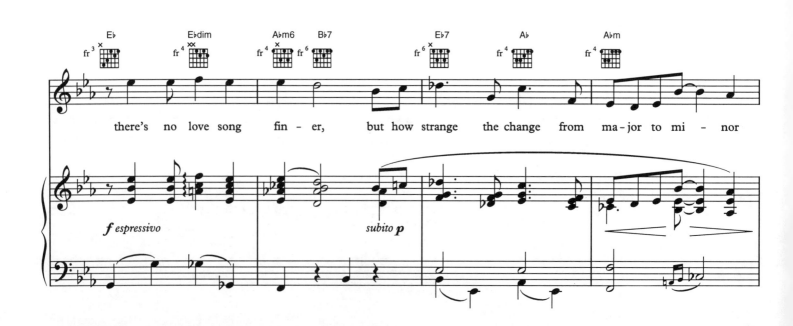

there's no love song fin - er, but how strange the change from ma-jor to mi - nor

Manhattan

Words by Lorenz Hart
Music by Richard Rodgers

The Lady Is A Tramp

Words by Lorenz Hart
Music by Richard Rodgers

Don't Explain

Words and Music by Arthur Hertzog Jnr and Billie Holiday

Slowly

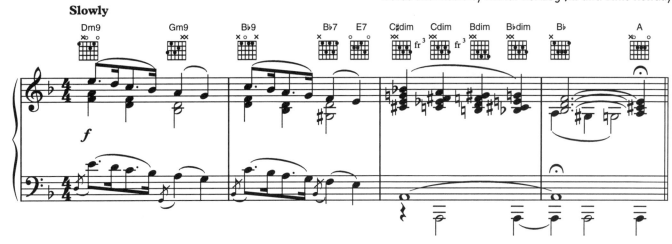

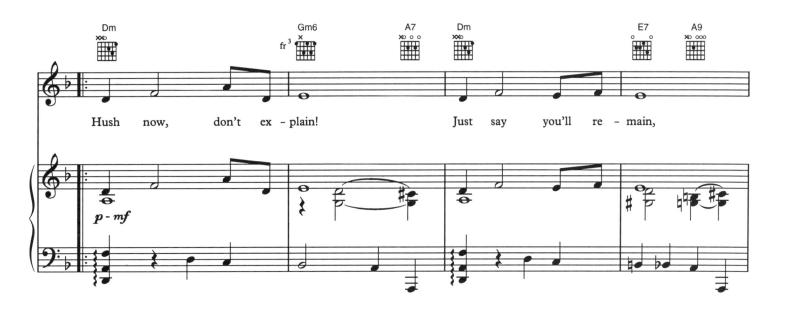

Hush now, don't ex - plain!   Just say you'll re - main,

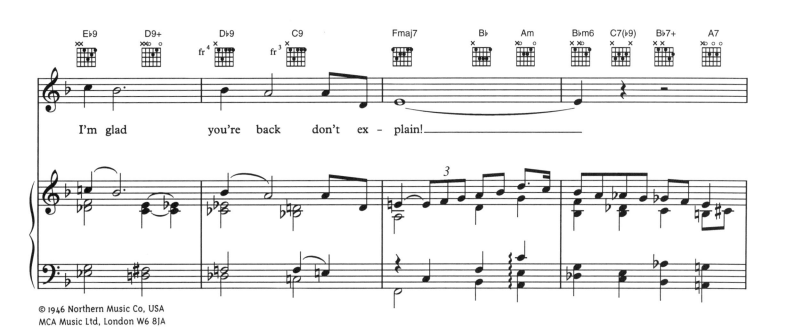

I'm glad you're back don't ex - plain!_____

Right or wrong don't mat-ter when you're with me, sweet. Hush now, don't ex -plain!

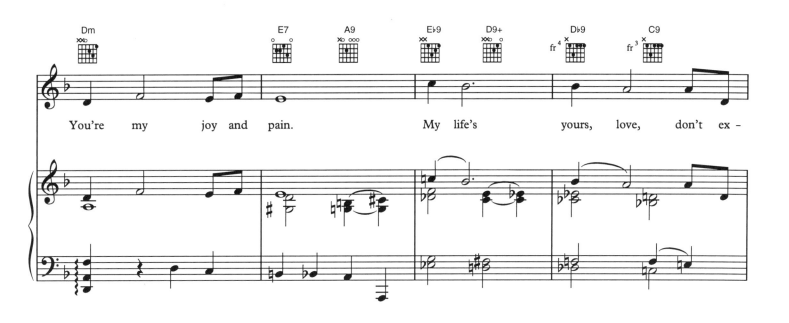

You're my joy and pain. My life's yours, love, don't ex -

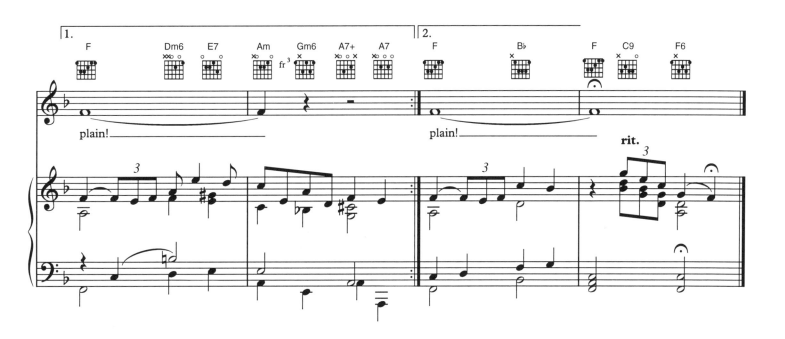

plain! plain!

rit.

Love Me Or Leave Me

Words by Gus Kahn
Music by Walter Donaldson

just rem - i - nis - cing, Re - gret - ting, in - stead of for - get -ting with some - bod - y else.

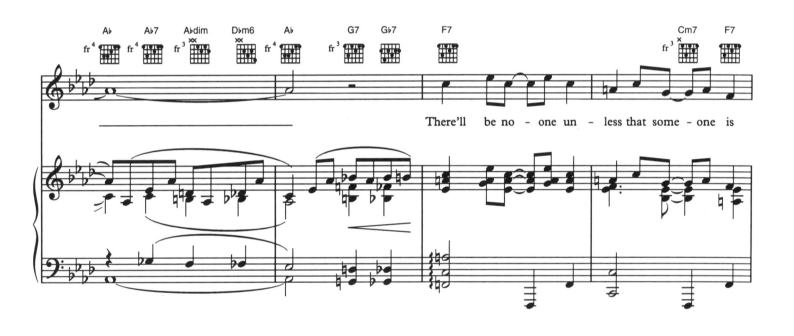

There'll be no - one un - less that some - one is

you;_____ I in - tend__ to be in - de - pen - dent - ly

blue.＿＿＿＿＿＿ I want your love, but I don't want to bor - row, To

have it to-day, and to give back to-mor - row; For my love is your love, there's no love for no-bod- y else!

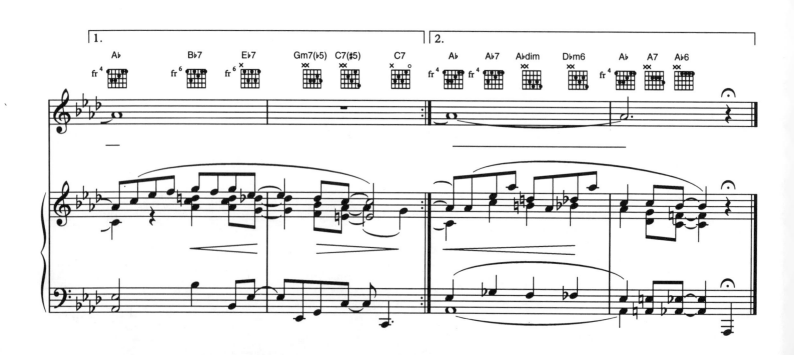

My Baby Just Cares For Me

Words by Gus Kahn
Music by Walter Donaldson

My ba - by don't care for cars and ra - ces, my ba - by don't care for high toned pla - ces. Liz Tay - lor is not his style and ev - en La - na Tur - ner's smile,

some - thing he can't___ see.__

My ba - by don't care___

who knows_____ it, my ba - by just cares

for me.

Little Girl Blue

Words by Lorenz Hart
Music by Richard Rodgers

64

Misty

Words by Johnny Burke
Music by Erroll Garner

Smoke Gets In Your Eyes

Words by Otto Harbach
Music by Jerome Kern

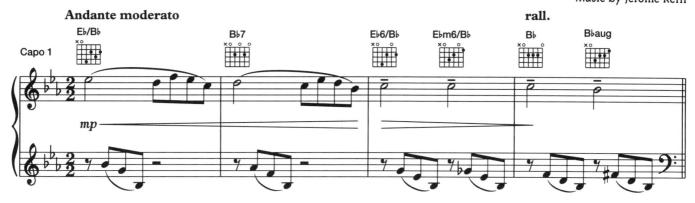

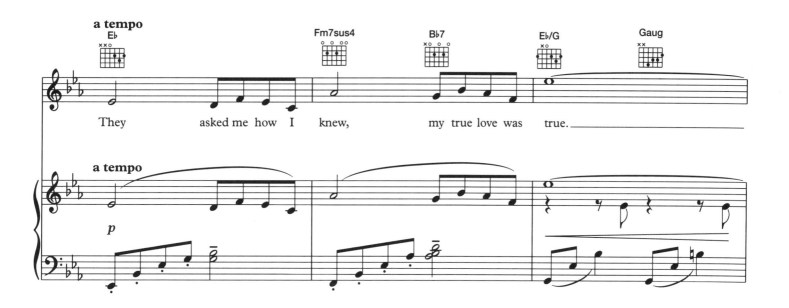

They asked me how I knew, my true love was true.___

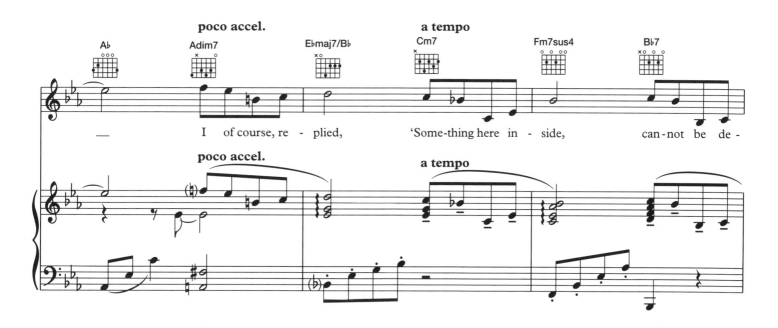

— I of course, re - plied, 'Some-thing here in - side, can-not be de -

All
The Woman Series

All Woman
volume one

Contents include: All Woman; Do You Know Where You're Going To?; Ev'ry Time We Say Goodbye;
Fever; I Am What I Am; I Will Always Love You; Miss You Like Crazy; Summertime;
Superwoman; What's Love Got To Do With It and Why Do Fools Fall In Love.
Order Ref: 19076

All Woman
volume two

Contents include: Don't It Make My Brown Eyes Blue; Giving You The Best That I Got;
Killing Me Softly With His Song; Memory; One Moment In Time; Pearl's A Singer;
That Ole Devil Called Love; Walk On By; The Wind Beneath My Wings and You Don't Have To Say You Love Me.
Order Ref: 2043A

All Woman
volume three

Contents include: Almaz; Big Spender; Crazy For You; Fame; The First Time Ever I Saw Your Face;
From A Distance; Love Letters; My Baby Just Cares For Me; My Funny Valentine; The Power Of Love;
Promise Me; Saving All My Love For You and Total Eclipse Of The Heart.
Order Ref: 2444A

All Woman
volume four

Contents include: Anything For You; Evergreen; For Your Eyes Only; I Will Survive; Mad About The Boy;
A Rainy Night in Georgia; Send In The Clowns; Smooth Operator; Sophisticated Lady; Stay With Me Till Dawn;
Sweet Love; Think Twice and Touch Me In The Morning.
Order Ref: 3034A

All Woman
Blues

Contents include: Body and Soul; Georgia On My Mind; God Bless' The Child;
I Don't Stand A Ghost Of A Chance With You; I Gotta Right To Sing The Blues; I'd Rather Go Blind;
Lover Man (Oh, Where Can You Be?); Mood Indigo; Stormy Weather and You've Changed.
Order Ref: 3690A

All Woman
Cabaret

Contents include: Almost Like Being In Love; Another Openin', Another Show; Anything Goes;
For Once In My Life; Goldfinger; I Won't Last A Day Without You; If My Friends Could See Me Now;
My Way; New York New York; People and There's No Business Like Show Business.
Order Ref: 3691A

All Woman
Jazz

Contents include: Bewitched; Crazy He Calls Me; A Foggy Day; Girl From Ipanema; How High The Moon;
I'm In The Mood For Love; It Don't Mean A Thing (If It Ain't Got That Swing); It's Only A Paper Moon;
Misty; On Green Dolphin Street; 'Round Midnight and Straighten Up And Fly Right.
Order Ref: 4778A